Pul...

**EU...**

Have you ever used the ... what it means? A G... Archimedes shouted it out in his bath one day when he discovered something very exciting. It means, 'I have found it', and you can use it when you've found out something really interesting or exciting, like all the information and amazing facts in this book!

*Eureka!* will help you find out about many topics such as Space, Dinosaurs, Ecology, Transport, Dolls and Clothes. It also gives you a list of museums around Great Britain that will help you discover even more about a wide variety of things such as the natural world, the history of your own area, inventions and discoveries – past, present and future!

The Museums Association commissioned a magazine called *Eureka!* which was published for children during Museums Year 1989. The editorial board consisted of eminent people from museums throughout the country and the patron of Museums Year was the Duchess of York. This book includes articles from the magazine as well as specially commissioned pieces.

Chris Meade is an anagram of another much more famous name. Can you mix up the letters and see what that famous name is?

Clue: It's a name that's just one word.

# Chris Meade

# EUREKA!
## Finding Out is Fun

### Illustrated by
# Jane Cope

PUFFIN BOOKS

PUFFIN BOOKS

Published by the Penguin Group
Penguin Books Ltd, 27 Wrights Lane, London W8 5TZ, England
Viking Penguin, a division of Penguin Books USA Inc.
375 Hudson Street, New York, New York 10014, USA
Penguin Books Australia Ltd, Ringwood, Victoria, Australia
Penguin Books Canada Ltd, 2801 John Street, Markham, Ontario, Canada L3R 1B4
Penguin Books (NZ) Ltd, 182–190 Wairau Road, Auckland 10, New Zealand

Penguin Books Ltd, Registered Offices: Harmondsworth, Middlesex, England

First published 1991
10 9 8 7 6 5 4 3 2 1

Design Partnership acknowledges the additional research
and material contributed by Camilla Boodle

Printed in England by Clays Ltd, St Ives plc

# CONTENTS

# WHAT IS A MUSEUM?

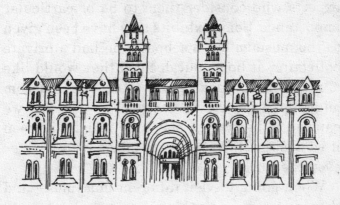

*T*he word 'museum' comes from the Greek word 'mouseion', which means 'of the muses'. This was a word given to special places dedicated to the goddesses of art and science. Each goddess had a group of followers who often gave her gifts, and these gifts made up the collections which were the earliest museums.

The oldest museum still in existence in the world is The Ashmolean in Oxford, which was built over three hundred years ago – between 1679 and 1683 – and named after the collector, Elias Ashmole. The largest and most visited museum in Great Britain is the British Museum, which was started in 1753 and opened to the public in 1759. Between three and four million people visit it every year!

7

Museums today often receive gifts to add to their collections. The exhibits you see when visiting them have usually been collected by experts who consider them to be of particular importance. Some exhibits may have been given to the museum by somebody who had a private collection at home but decided they would like a museum to look after it, or one museum might lend objects to another. In this way we can see things which may only usually be seen if we visited different parts of the country – or even the world!

When going to visit different museums – and there is a new one opening somewhere every 18 days – you can learn about many things such as the history of where you live, or of another civilization like the ancient Egyptians. You can also look at plants and animals from the natural world, find out about art, science and technology and learn what progress has been made over the centuries.

As you will discover, museums cover a wide range of subjects. Many museums have 'hands-on' galleries, where every exhibit is an experiment or demonstration which visitors can take part in and discover for themselves. There are also many 'working' museums where the exhibits are in everyday use in their natural surroundings.

Museums cater for everyone – they have never been more exciting and popular and they

are there for us all to enjoy! The following chapters of this book will give you a taster of what's on offer and make you want to find out more so that you too can shout 'eureka!' – I've found it!

# DINOSAURS

*D*inosaurs are mysterious creatures that lived long before us. It is hard to imagine what life was like 265 million years ago when dinosaurs dominated the Earth. We know about dinosaurs from the fossils of their bones and teeth and from the remains of their skeletons. By looking at their teeth we can find out what they ate – worn, flattened teeth mean that a dinosaur lived off plants that needed chewing; sharp, blade-like teeth mean a diet of meat.

The word dinosaur means 'terrible lizard', coming from two Greek words 'dinos' (terrible) and 'sauros' (lizard). They were related to today's reptiles (e.g. crocodiles and lizards). They had scaly skins and produced their off-spring by laying eggs. Dinosaurs lived on land and were able to walk and run, though some were so heavy and large that they moved very slowly. Stegosaurus was a large dinosaur which had to stay in one place eating all the time just to stay alive!

We still have a lot to learn about dinosaurs. There are about 800 different species known so far and new ones are being discovered all the time. For example, in 1983 a keen fossil hunter called Mr Walker was exploring a clay pit near his home in Surrey. He found an enormous old claw bone which scientists told him was part of a dinosaur which had lived 124 million years ago. Because Mr Walker had found the bone, the dinosaur was named after him 'Baryonyx Walkeri', which means 'Walker's Heavy Claw'. The claw bone is now on display at the Natural History Museum in London.

---

**FACT**

The first complete skeleton of a dinosaur was found in Dorset by a 12-year-old girl called Mary Anning in 1811. Perhaps *you* might find a fossil or part of a dinosaur!

---

The best known of all the dinosaurs is Tyrannosaurus rex, which weighed up to 10 tonnes and was the biggest of all the dinosaurs. It had huge jaws and sharp teeth and six giant talons on its back feet for killing its prey.

Other well-known dinosaurs include Triceratops, which was over 8 metres long. A modern

rhinoceros has only one horn but Triceratops
had three protruding from the front of its head!

Diplodocus was a huge dinosaur nearly 30
metres long, but it had a brain that was no

bigger than a rabbit's. Being amphibious, and therefore at home on both land and water, it spent its time in and around marshes and swamps.

We still don't know why dinosaurs became extinct. One theory is that the earth's climate changed and that dinosaurs could not survive. However, even today we can see some animals that evolved from the dinosaurs of the past. Archaeopteryx, the first bird, was the direct descendant of small flesh-eating dinosaurs, and iguanas and crocodiles are similar to the ancient reptiles.

### Did you know?

- The last of the dinosaurs died out 65 million years ago and the earliest primitive people did not live before 1 million years ago. Dinosaurs were around long before we were!

- Some animals that we think have died out turn out not to have done so. For example, a fish called a coelacanth, which was around at the time of the dinosaurs, was thought by scientists to be extinct until an African fisherman caught one in 1938. The coelacanth, covered in bright blue scales, had not changed over a period of 300 million years! There is a coelacanth display and film in the Natural History Museum in London.

**Museums where you can find out more about dinosaurs:**

Bristol Museum, Victoria Street, Bristol

Dinosaur Museum, Dorchester, Dorset

Hancock Museum, Newcastle upon Tyne

Hunterian Museum, Glasgow, Scotland

Liverpool Museum, William Brown Street, Liverpool

National Museum of Wales, Cathays Park, Cardiff, Wales

Natural History Museum, Exhibition Road, London SW7

Royal Museum of Scotland, Chambers Street, Edinburgh, Scotland

Ulster Museum, Botanic Gardens, Belfast, Northern Ireland

# NATURAL HISTORY AND ECOLOGY

*E*cology is the study of plants and animals in their own home or habitat. Plants and animals, from tiny insects to huge animals like elephants and whales, all live in a way of life that is called an 'ecosystem'. All these creatures need one another in order to survive, so when humans hunt and kill them many of the species cannot survive and some will become extinct, which means they will die out.

Today we know about the dangers of upsetting the ecosystem. The conservation (or Green) movement is teaching us to understand the Earth and its inhabitants and to care properly for it.

The Earth is a varied planet. Some regions of the world are hot and dry, some are hot and wet, others are cold. Different plants and animals are found in different parts of the world.

The deserts of the world are very hot and dry. Only plants and animals that do not need much water can live here. Desert animals include the camel, and the most common desert plant is the cactus.

---

**FACT**

The camel is known as the 'Ship of the Desert', as it can carry heavy loads and walk for long distances without needing to drink water.

---

The tropical rain forest consists of large areas of forest near the Equator where there is lots of rainfall and high temperatures. The trees grow very tall and many birds, insects and plants are able to live in this warm, wet climate. Today the rainforest is being cut down to provide wood for shelter and the habitat of these animals and plants is being threatened.

In Britain, where the summers are warm and the winters cold, the trees shed their leaves every year. These are called 'deciduous' trees. In colder regions nearer the North and South Poles, where it is cold throughout the year, the trees are called 'coniferous', or 'evergreen', as they do not shed their leaves.

Large areas of the world consist of grassland where crops are grown and animals graze. In North America there are huge prairies where wheat is grown for flour – this area is called the 'bread basket of the world'.

In all these areas of the world there is an ecosystem with animals and plants living together. In each ecosystem there is a food-chain. Plants provide food for plant-eating animals, or herbivores (such as cows), and they in turn provide food for meat-eating animals, or carnivores (such as humans). So plants form the first step in the food-chain and humans form the last step.

The sea is also an ecosystem with its own food-chain. Seaweed and plankton on the

17

surface of the sea provide food for fish living in the sea. If we poison the fish in the sea, we risk poisoning ourselves.

---

**FACT**

In Africa, a fish from Egypt, called the Nile Perch, was put into Lake Victoria in Tanzania, but it ate up all the other fish in the lake. Therefore, it upset the ecosystem.

---

Our modern way of life causes damage to the ecosystem by pollution.

In Japan, a poison called mercury was dumped into the sea from a factory. The mercury was eaten by fish in the sea. When the fish were caught and eaten by villagers many of them became very ill with mercury poisoning.

We dirty the air we breathe with chemicals from factories and fumes from the exhaust pipes of cars. A poisonous gas called sulphur dioxide causes 'acid rain'. If there is poison in the air when it rains, trees and plants will be damaged. Many countries in the world have now agreed to try and stop acid rain.

We are causing harm to human beings by damaging the 'ozone layer' which surrounds the Earth. It is like a blanket which stops us from being burnt by the sun's rays.

Scientists have told us to stop attacking the ozone layer with poisonous fumes otherwise we will damage our skin.

Rivers and lakes become dirty when chemicals are dumped in them. Fish and plants die. Oil spilled into the sea from oil tankers kills sea animals and sea birds.

Human beings and animals have shared the Earth for thousands of years. However, many species of animals are now in danger. Either they have been hunted for meat or for their skins, or their habitats have been destroyed and there is nowhere for them to live.

One of the animals in danger is the elephant. There are two types of elephant, the Indian and the African. Elephants are intelligent animals

and have been used for hundreds of years in India and Burma to work in forests. However, the elephant is in danger from people who want to kill it in order to cut off its ivory tusks.

---

**FACT**

Scientists who have studied the behaviour of elephants believe they are much cleverer than either dogs or horses!

---

Jaguars and tigers are both hunted for their skins, which have beautiful markings. It is believed that there are fewer than 2,000 tigers left in India.

---

**FACT**

The cheetah is one of the fastest animals on land. In ancient Persia, hunters used to carry cheetahs on horseback with them when they went out hunting and send them after prey.

---

Mountain gorillas live in dense forests on the slopes of mountains in central Africa. They are in danger from poachers, who kill them, and from farmers, who are cutting down the trees and clearing the forests in order to graze animals.

The okapi is a rare animal that looks like a cross between a zebra and a giraffe. It is found only in a country called Zaire, in central Africa, where it lives in the rainforest. If the forest is cut down the okapi will not survive.

### Did you know?

- In Sweden, woodpeckers are rare because they like to build their nests in old and hollow trees and these are being cut down.

- Humans have been responsible for destroying several species of birds. One of these was the dodo, a large bird rather like a turkey, which could not fly. Sailors discovered dodos on the island of Mauritius and killed and ate them. The last one died in 1681.

● It is not just important for animals and birds that their habitat survives. Human beings need plants for medicines. Digitalis is a drug made from part of the foxglove plant, which is given to people with heart disease.

Everyone can become an ecologist and study the world around us. Plan a project around the ecosystem in your garden or in the local park. Send off for information from organizations such as the World Wide Fund for Nature.

**Museums where you can find out more about natural history and ecology:**

Buxton Micrarium, Buxton, Derbyshire

Geological Museum, Exhibition Road, London SW7

Kendal Museum of Natural History and Archaeology,
   Kendal, Cumbria

Liverpool Museum (Natural History Centre), William
   Brown Street, Liverpool

Manchester Museum, Oxford Road, Manchester

National Museum of Wales, Cathays Park, Cardiff,
   Wales

Natural History Museum, Exhibition Road, London
   SW7

Royal Museum of Scotland, Chambers Street,
   Edinburgh, Scotland

Ulster Museum, Botanic Gardens, Belfast, Northern
   Ireland

## ECO QUIZ

*T*ry to spot all the 'Coastal Wildlife' on the left in the picture of this seashore scene and say which of the 'Coastal Dangers' affects each of them. Check your answers below.

COASTAL
WILDLIFE

Crab

Shrimp

Little Tern

Butterfly

Anemone

Seal

Eggs

butterflies that live among them. Catching butterflies with a net will almost certainly harm them. A washed-up fishing-net and broken fishing-line can entangle birds, seals and crabs. Plastic bags are dangerous to birds when swallowed. Can you think of any other dangers?

## Answers

Oil and petrol from leaking drums affect everything in the sea and on the shore. Stepping carelessly can crush shrimps and birds' eggs. Broken glass can damage birds' legs. In sunny weather, a glass bottle can start a fire, endangering wild flowers and the

Plastic Bag

Broken Glass

Fishing Net

Butterfly Net

Glass Bottle

Careless Foot

Leaking Drum

COASTAL DANGERS

# PHOTOGRAPHY, FILM AND TELEVISION

## PHOTOGRAPHY

*O*ne of the most important scientific discoveries of all time was the discovery of photography. Without photography and cameras we would have no cinema or television, no video or photocopy or X-ray machines. In the past, people who wanted pictures of themselves had to pay a painter to paint an oil picture, but today, thanks to the camera, we can all have pictures of our families and friends.

For many hundreds of years, scientists tried to find a way to take pictures of the world around them. The first photograph was taken in 1826 by a Frenchman called Niepce, who managed to make a picture of the view from his bedroom window appear on a pewter plate. However, putting photographs on plates was not a very practical process! The next steps were taken by a Frenchman, Louis Daguerre, and an Englishman, William Henry Fox Talbot. Fox Talbot discovered a way of making 'negatives', which is still the way photographs are taken today. However, taking photographs was a very slow process. The cameras were very big and heavy and the person being photographed had to sit still for a long time while the picture was being taken, unlike today when it takes a few seconds.

---

**FACT**

An American inventor called George Eastman invented the first roll of film, which was named the Kodak film. As a result, large cameras were no longer needed, and smaller, lighter and cheaper ones were developed. Today you can easily fit a camera into your pocket.

---

## How the camera works

The camera works in the same way that the human eye works. Light comes into the camera through the lens. The lens makes an image (a picture) on the film in the camera. When you press the camera button, a shutter opens to let light on to the film to take the picture. On dark days you will need more light to take a picture

than on bright, sunny ones. If you have an automatic camera, the shutter speed and the amount of light is judged for you and all you do is press the button. The lenses on some cameras can be changed according to the type of picture you want to take. A wide-angled lens gives a wide view. If you want to take something far away, a telephoto lens gives a close-up view, like a telescope.

When you have taken a number of pictures and used up all the film in the camera, the film is developed. The first stage is the negative, when you get lots of small pictures on strips of film. On the negative, the picture is in reverse, with the dark parts of the picture looking light and the light ones dark. To make the print, light is shone through the negative, which is printed on special coated paper.

## FILM

Once photography had been developed, film-making soon followed. In France, two brothers, Auguste and Louis Lumière, working in their father's photographic factory, invented a machine called a 'cinematographe'. They showed the first film to the public in Paris in 1895.

---

**FACT**

The first films were shot in black and white and had no sound. They had to be short, because the first projectors could not cope with long pieces of film. Sometimes films were accompanied by piano music or by a full orchestra!

---

Films had to be made out of doors because indoor lighting was not bright enough for the cameras. One of the reasons why the film industry in America developed in Hollywood in California, was because it had a very good, dry climate, with lots of sunshine and very little rain.

Old films look rather jerky to us today. This is because cameras were mounted on tripods and could not be moved very easily. Today's modern cameras are mounted on wheeled platforms or 'dollies', and can be moved to wherever they are needed.

Films soon became very popular and film stars of the 'silent screen', as it was known, such as Charlie Chaplin and Laurel and Hardy, were very successful. Between 1905 and 1910, 200 cinemas were built in London alone! When sound for films was invented in 1929, the cinema became even more popular. These new films were called 'talkies'. Today films are made and shown all over the world either in cinemas or on television and video.

## TELEVISION

The invention of television came after the invention of film. In Britain, television was first demonstrated by a Scotsman called John Logie Baird in 1926. The first television service to

viewers in Britain began in 1936 with transmissions from the Alexandra Palace studios in London.

Television works by sending pictures through cables to a transmitting station. From there they are carried on radio waves, which are picked up by individual television aerials on people's houses. The signals are changed back into pictures and sound and shown on the TV screen in the home. By 'bouncing' signals off special satellites, TV signals can be sent over very long distances.

---

**FACT**

In 1936 television sets cost between £60 and £120 – about half the price of a small car! They could only be bought by very few people. During the Second World War, television services were stopped, but were restarted after the war with coverage of the Olympic Games held in London in 1948. As sets became cheaper, television became more popular and nowadays only about 4% of households do NOT have a television set.

---

In the early days of television, programmes were presented 'live', but since the development of video tape, most programmes are pre-recorded, though news and current events are still done on the spot. Video is a way of recording pictures and sounds on magnetic tape.

Videos can be shown on televisions at home and are also used in schools and hospitals. A sports team can watch a video of their game to look at their mistakes in order to correct them. TV and video cameras are used in some shops and banks to monitor what is going on as a security measure. This is called 'closed-circuit' television.

### Did you know?

● Televisions are getting smaller all the time. Now you can get ones that are pocket-sized or even wrist-watch-sized, though this means that you can hardly see the picture!

**Museums where you can find out more about
photography, film and television:**

Design Museum, Butler's Wharf, Shad Thames,
London SE1

Exploratory Hands-On Science Centre, Temple
Meads, Bristol

Fox Talbot Museum, Lacock, Wiltshire

Greater Manchester Museum of Science and
Industry, Liverpool Road, Manchester

Museum of the History of Science, Broad Street,
Oxford

Museum of the Moving Image, South Bank Centre,
Waterloo, London SE1

National Museum of Photography, Film and
Television, Prince's View, Bradford, West
Yorkshire (includes the IMAX cinema, the biggest
cinema screen in Britain!)

Photographers' Gallery, Great Newport Street,
London WC1

Science Museum, Exhibition Road, London SW7

Victoria and Albert Museum, Exhibition Road,
London SW7

# TELEPHONES

*T*he telephone was invented by Alexander Graham Bell, who was born in Edinburgh in 1847. He specialized in sound and taught people who found speaking difficult or had never learned to speak. At the age of 23 he emigrated to Canada and later became an American citizen . . .

1895: MANY VICTORIAN HANDSETS WERE BEAUTIFUL, ELEGANT AND FUNCTIONAL.

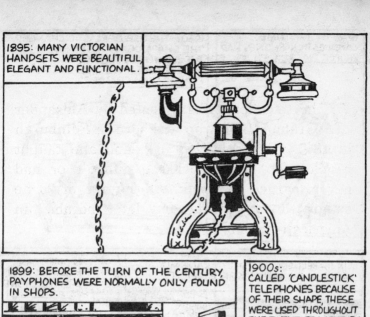

1899: BEFORE THE TURN OF THE CENTURY, PAYPHONES WERE NORMALLY ONLY FOUND IN SHOPS.

1900s: CALLED 'CANDLESTICK' TELEPHONES BECAUSE OF THEIR SHAPE, THESE WERE USED THROUGHOUT THE TWENTIETH CENTURY. HOWEVER, THE HANDSETS OFTEN PROVED TO BE FAR FROM SUCCESSFUL.

1914-1918: DURING THE FIRST WORLD WAR, FIELD TELEPHONES PROVED INVALUABLE.

**1924: BY THIS TIME, 'CANDLESTICK' PHONES HAD PROPER DIALS.**

**1930s: THE USE OF PLASTIC CHANGED THE SHAPE OF MANY THINGS—INCLUDING THE TELEPHONE. A NEW MICROPHONE MADE THE HANDSET PRACTICAL ONCE MORE.**

**THE '999' EMERGENCY TELEPHONE SERVICE CAME INTO OPERATION.**

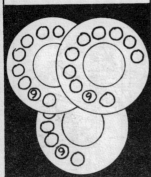

**THE RED 'JUBILEE' TELEPHONE KIOSK (OR BOX) WAS INTRODUCED. A FEW STILL REMAIN TODAY.**

**1940s: THE TELEPHONE HAD AN INTERNAL BELL FOR THE FIRST TIME.**

**1950s: WALL TELEPHONES WITH HANDSETS WERE USEFUL SPACE-SAVERS.**

1960s: THE LIGHTWEIGHT PLASTIC TELEPHONES HAD IMPROVED CIRCUITRY AND A CLEAN, FUNCTIONAL SHAPE.

1970s: THE TRIMPHONE MARKED THE END OF THE IDEA OF A 'STANDARD' TELEPHONE. AS WELL AS A REVOLUTIONARY SHAPE, IT HAD AN ILLUMINATED DIAL AND VARIABLE ELECTRONIC CALLER.

1980s: THE SLIMTEL 10 ONE-PIECE TELEPHONE.

PUSH-BUTTON TELEPHONE FOR HOME OR OFFICE.

THE CORDLESS TELEPHONE GIVING MOBILITY A SHORT DISTANCE FROM BASE.

PAYPHONES CATER FOR ALL SECTIONS OF THE COMMUNITY.

THE CELLNET TELEPHONE IS COMPLETELY MOBILE.

FACSIMILE MACHINES RELAY MESSAGES VIA THE WRITTEN WORD.

THERE ARE MANY WORKING EXHIBITS AND DISPLAYS AT THE TELECOM TECHNOLOGY SHOWCASE IN LONDON.

# COMPUTERS

*A* computer is an electronic machine which handles information and makes calculations. In just a few seconds computers can do millions of calculations that would take people weeks or even years to do. Computers have been developed this century and we are the first generation of people to use computers in our everyday lives.

We have always needed machines to help us count and add up figures. The ancient Egyptians, Greeks and Romans used a device called the abacus, which was a frame with wooden or wire bars fixed across it. Beads were moved along the bars to make calculations. The Incas of Peru kept count of their animals and harvests by tying knots in cords or ropes, called quipus.

Throughout the ages, scientists tried to invent counting machines. In the nineteenth century, an Englishman called Charles Babbage attempted to develop the first computer, which he called an 'analytical engine'. However, it was not until the Second World War that computers were developed. In 1943 the first computer was built in Britain. It was used to crack German secret codes and was called 'Colossus'.

The first computers which were built in the 1950s were very large, often needing whole rooms to house them. They were expensive to make and to look after. The breakthrough in the computer industry came as the result of a revolution in electronics. In the 1960s, a device called a 'silicon chip' was developed. Now it was possible to make cheaper, smaller and more powerful computers. The silicon chip is the 'brain' of the computer and may be as small as a thumb-nail and yet store more information than the human brain!

There are now several different sizes of computer, but they all work in the same way. The parts of the computer machinery are called the 'hardware' and the special programs that tell the computer what to do are called the 'software'. The program gives the computer instructions since, unlike a human being, it cannot think for itself but can only do what we tell it to do. The information that we put into a computer is called 'data'. It is stored in the computer's memory until we need it. Computers are able to store huge amounts of information that would fill thousands of sheets of paper if it was all written down. This is why computers are so useful to banks and hospitals, which have to deal with lots of people and keep their records.

The largest computers are called 'mainframes' and store huge amounts of data. 'Minicomputers' are smaller than mainframes and are used for smaller jobs. 'Microcomputers' are the portable computers that people have at home or in the office. A microcomputer can be linked by a telephone to a big mainframe computer so that information can be passed to it. This is called a 'network'. You might want to find out from your local travel agent whether you can go on holiday to Spain next week. The travel agent's computer is linked to a central computer which will be able to tell you immediately whether there are still seats on the

plane and rooms in the hotel you want to stay in. If you book the holiday, your booking is entered on to the travel agent's computer and transferred to the mainframe so that the information remains up to date for the next customer.

---

**FACT**

Information can be passed between computers in different countries by means of communications satellites in orbit high above the Earth.

---

## Computers in everyday life

New uses are being developed for computers all the time. Here are some ways in which they are already used:

In hospitals computers are used to monitor the condition (e.g. the heartbeat) of people who are ill.

Shops use computers to keep a record of what has been bought and sold – this is called 'stock control'.

Central and local government use computers to keep a record of when we pay our taxes, rents, licences and other bills.

Computers help designers, architects and engineers to design buildings and products such as cars. This is called computer-aided design or CAD.

Automatic cameras have tiny computers built into them. In a split second they calculate the correct setting for the camera when you want to take a picture so that you get a perfect picture.

Central-heating systems, washing-machines, burglar alarms and supermarket check-outs all use tiny computers in their operations.

## Into the future

Letters are now being sent from one computer to another by telephone since it is quicker than sending them by post.

Television screens at home are being linked

to computers by telephone lines. You can call up information on your TV screen. In a few years' time we will be able to shop from home without having to visit the shops at all.

Video discs may become the books of the future. They can store the same information as books do and take up much less space. The video disc is linked to a computer screen which shows you the pages of words and pictures.

## Robots

Robots are machines controlled by computers which can be programmed to perform certain mechanical tasks. They are often used to do tasks that are dangerous for human beings: for example, exploring deep beneath the surface of the sea or going into space. They are also used in factories to do boring tasks. The motor car industry uses robots for simple jobs such as welding, painting and tightening screws. However, robots will never replace humans since they cannot think for themselves but always have to be told what to do.

# Did you know?

- Computers can be used to train airline pilots. Machines called simulators are used. It is much better for pilots to learn on a machine since if they make a mistake they have not caused an accident which might be dangerous and expensive.

- Computers help solve crime! If a police officer sees something suspicious he or she can call up a database of information and have, for example, a car number-plate checked. This will give the name of the owner and help the police officer find out if the car is stolen.

**Museums where you can find out more about computers:**

Catalyst, Widnes, Lancashire

Greater Manchester Museum of Science and
    Industry, Liverpool Road, Manchester

Science Museum, Exhibition Road, London SW7

# TRAINS

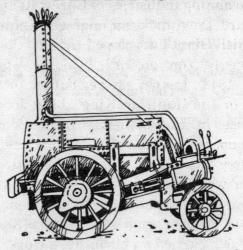

*T*rains are used to transport passengers and goods from one destination to another. They consist of a series of carriages or trucks drawn by an engine along lengths of metal tracks. The first 'trains' did not have engines – instead, horses were used to pull loads. During the eighteenth century, when Britain was at war with France (1793–1815), there was a shortage of horses and another source of power to pull loads had to be found. In fact, a steam-powered locomotive had been built by a Frenchman called Nicholas Cugnot as early as 1771. However, the engine that he built went out of control as it was being demonstrated and a number of spectators were injured. Instead of being hailed as a hero, Cugnot was sent to prison!

In Britain the first steam-engines were used in the mining industries of Cornwall and Wales. Richard Trevithick, an engineer known as the 'Cornish Giant', developed the first steam locomotive to run on rails. George Stephenson (1781–1848), known as the 'Father of the Railway' or the 'Railway King', built locomotives for use in the collieries of Yorkshire and Durham. He realized that trains could be used to carry passengers and the first railway line, which was built between Stockton and Darlington, was opened on 27 September 1825. George Stephenson's son, Robert Stephenson (1803–59), carried on his father's work, building the famous locomotive, Rocket (1829), for the Manchester–Liverpool line, the first public railway. The National Railway Museum at York has the remains of the original Rocket on display.

---

**FACT**

The first British monarch to travel by train was Queen Victoria in 1842.

---

It took people some time to get used to trains. When they first started travelling through the countryside, it was believed that they would frighten animals and poison crops. Travelling in the early trains was not very comfortable. You only got a roof over your head if you could afford to go first-class. Second- and third-class passengers were in the open air and had to put up their umbrellas if it rained!

Many railways were built in the nineteenth century. The men responsible for cutting the line and laying the track were called 'navvies', from the word 'navigator'. Bridges had to be built to carry trains over rivers and valleys. Many of these were masterpieces of engineering and construction. For example, the Forth Bridge, crossing the Firth of Forth in Scotland (opened in 1890), employed 5,000 men. 54,000 tons of steel and six and a half million rivets were used in its construction.

Every country in Europe began to build railways. In America, the first line to cross the whole country was opened in 1869. The Canadian Pacific Railway, which included 2,500 miles (4,025 km.) of line, was opened in 1885. The journey from Montreal to Vancouver, which took five months by horse-drawn coach on the road, took only five days by train!

---

**FACT**

The highest railways in the world are in South America. A branch of the Peruvian Central Railway reaches 4,500 metres at one point in the Andes mountains.

---

The railway companies competed with each other to provide a fast, reliable service. Sleeping and restaurant cars were added to the train to make the journey more comfortable. The Flying Scotsman, which travelled between London and Edinburgh, even had a cocktail bar and a hairdressing salon! One of the most famous trains in Europe was the Orient Express,

which went three times a week from Paris in France to Istanbul in Turkey, covering 1,750 miles (2,820 km.) in 65 hours. The train was so well known that the famous writer Agatha Christie even wrote a crime mystery set on the train called *Murder on the Orient Express*.

With the development of the diesel engine this century, the age of steam came to an end. The last British Rail steam locomotive was built at Swindon in 1960. Now, many modern trains are run on electricity. But you can see many old locomotives in museums, and there are still stretches of track where you can travel by steam train. These include the Didcot Railway Centre in Oxfordshire, the Bluebell Railway in Sussex and the Bressingham Live Steam Museum in Norfolk.

**Did you know?**

- The longest railway in the world is the Trans-Siberian Railway, which crosses the USSR from Moscow to Vladivostock, a distance of 5,801 miles (9,340 km.). The Trans-Siberian express train takes 9 days 3 hours to complete the journey.

- The world's largest railway station is the Grand Central Terminal in New York, which has 44 platforms.

- The first underground railway in the world was opened in London in 1863.

**Museums where you can find out more about trains:**

Darlington Railway Centre and Museum, Darlington, Co. Durham

Greater Manchester Museum of Science and Industry, Liverpool Road, Manchester

Museum of Transport, Glasgow, Scotland

National Railway Museum, Leeman Road, York

Science Museum, Exhibition Road, London SW7

Springburn Museum and Exhibition Centre, Ayr Street, Glasgow, Scotland

Welsh Industrial and Maritime Museum, Cardiff, Wales

# SHIPS

*M*ost of the earth's surface is covered by water. There are inland rivers and lakes and huge oceans and seas separating one land mass from another. From the earliest times there had to be ways of navigating these waters so that people could explore.

The very first boats were simple – either a hollowed-out tree trunk (not very different in shape from a modern canoe) or an animal skin stretched over a frame in the shape of a large wooden basket. These boats were paddled with wooden paddles. The Peruvians of South America used a very light wood called balsa-wood to make rafts. In ancient Egypt, boats were made of papyrus reeds.

---

**FACT**

The first known picture of a sailing ship is on a 5,000-year-old Egyptian vase.

---

The Greeks and Romans developed elaborate wooden warships, called galleys, which had 'banks' of oars to make them go as fast as possible. Slaves were used to row these heavy boats – a Greek 'trireme' (meaning it had three banks of oars) had about 170 rowers who rowed in time to a man playing the flute!

These early boats relied on muscle power to make them travel, but it was realized that wind power could make the boat go faster. Boats were built with masts and sails which could travel further. The Vikings of the eighth century were great seafarers, travelling from their homes in Denmark, Norway and Sweden to Britain, France, Ireland, Greece, Spain and Russia to trade and plunder. We know a lot about Viking ships, as it was the custom to bury a chief in his ship when he died and some have been discovered, the most famous being the 'Gokstad' ship now on display in Norway. At the British Museum in London there is a carved prow of a Viking ship – a very savage head with rows of teeth!

The fifteenth century was a time of scientific invention and discovery. Explorers from European countries went in search of new lands. In 1497, Vasco da Gama sailed to India and in 1522 another Portuguese, Ferdinand Magellan, sailed around the world.

In 1580, Sir Francis Drake, an English explorer, did the same. The English navy had

been expanded by Queen Elizabeth I and it was thanks to Drake and his men that the Spanish Armada was defeated in 1588. The *Mary Rose* is a Tudor warship which was rescued from the sea and restored. You can see it at Portsmouth, where it is on permanent display.

Captain Cook was an English explorer who 'discovered' Australia, New Zealand and New Guinea over two hundred years ago. The Captain Cook Birthplace Museum at Middlesbrough in Cleveland contains many items associated with his life and voyages.

In the eighteenth and nineteenth centuries, the British navy was the best in the world. In 1805, Nelson defeated the combined French and Spanish fleets at the Battle of Trafalgar and put an end to Napoleon's plans to invade England. Nelson's ship, the *Victory*, was built from

2,500 oak trees and had 104 guns. It had 842 sailors on board! The *Victory* is also on display at Portsmouth naval base.

---

**FACT**

On fighting ships like Nelson's *Victory* there were several boys on board. They were called 'powder monkeys' because it was their job to keep the gun crews supplied with cartridges of gunpowder.

---

As trade between countries developed, it was a challenge to see who could build the fastest ships. In America in the nineteenth century, clippers were built. The first British clippers brought tea from China to London. They were called the 'tea clippers'. Clippers were also used to bring wool and grain from Australia.

One of the fastest clippers, the *Cutty Sark*, could sail from Australia to England in a record 69 days. The *Cutty Sark* forms part of the displays of the National Maritime Museum at Greenwich in London.

With the invention of the steam-engine and the building of iron steamships, the age of the clipper ended. Once ships had engines they did not need the wind, and could go further and faster. The British engineer Isambard Kingdom Brunel built the *Great Western* in 1837, which was the first steamship to cross the Atlantic Ocean. In 1897 the first turbine engine was developed by Sir Charles Parsons. The ship, the *Turbinia*, which he designed is now on display as part of Newcastle's Museums of Science and Engineering.

The first steam turbo passenger liner was launched in 1904. Many luxury liners carried passengers and mail across the Atlantic. The most luxurious liner of them all, the *Titanic*, was launched in 1912. It was claimed that the *Titanic* was unsinkable, but on her first voyage to America she hit an iceberg which ripped a hole in her hull and she sank, in one of the worst disasters this century. 1,490 passengers and crew were drowned. Today we find it quicker and easier to fly by aeroplane to America.

Although planes have replaced passenger liners, we still use ships for many different purposes. For example, we have cargo ships such as oil tankers, warships for navies (including aircraft carriers, which are so big that planes and helicopters can land on their flight decks) and working ships on canals and rivers, carrying goods. In Britain most of our goods are now carried by road or rail, but many people enjoy going on an old-fashioned canal boat to explore the countryside.

## Did you know?

- Today it is easy for sailors out at sea to communicate with other boats since they have powerful radios. Before radio, flags were used. It did not matter if sailors did not understand each other's language, since there was (and still is) an International Code of Signals using 40 flags in different combinations.

- Children living on canal boats were in charge of making sure that the horse pulling the boat walked steadily and did not slow down. They only went to school when the boat was tied up for any length of time!

- The Ellesmere Port Boat Museum, near Liverpool, has a collection of over 50 canal and river boats. Many are being restored, and visitors can see traditional boat-building techniques still being used.

**Museums where you can find out more about ships:**

Boat Museum, Ellesmere Port, Cheshire

Brunel's SS *Great Britain*, once the world's largest iron ship, has been restored and is at the Great Western Dock, Bristol

Chatham Historic Dockyard, Chatham, Kent

Exeter Maritime Museum, Exeter, Devon

Falmouth Maritime Museum, Falmouth, Cornwall

HMS *Belfast*, a Second World War cruiser (now part of the Imperial War Museum) permanently moored by Tower Bridge, London

HMS *Victory*, *Mary Rose* and Royal Naval Museum, all at HM Naval Base, Portsmouth, Hants

Merseyside Maritime Museum, Albert Dock, Liverpool

National Maritime Museum, Greenwich, London SE10

National Waterways Museum, Gloucester

Science Museum, Exhibition Road, London SW7

Scottish Maritime Museum, Irvine, Scotland

Town Docks Museum, Hull, Humberside

Welsh Industrial and Maritime Museum, Cardiff, Wales

# SPACE – THE LAST FRONTIER

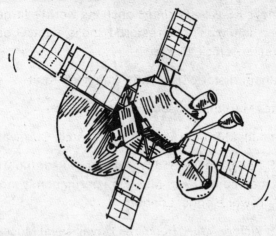

*T*he story of space exploration is a very short one, but its origins can be traced back to the East, probably China, where a thousand years ago it was known how to make fireworks.

By 1300, black powder and rockets were common in both Arabia and Europe and used not only as fireworks, but also as weapons.

In the nineteenth century, such authors as Jules Verne and H. G. Wells were adding knowledge to traditional tales of travelling to other planets, in what became known as science fiction.

Great advances in rocket technology continued into the twentieth century, when fiction became fact . . .

ON 12th APRIL 1961, YURI GAGARIN BECAME THE FIRST MAN IN SPACE... AND YET AGAIN AMERICA HAD COME SECOND IN THE SPACE RACE — BUT THEIR DETERMINATION WAS EVEN GREATER!

SOON AFTER, PRESIDENT JOHN F. KENNEDY DELIVERED A HISTORIC SPEECH...

AMERICA WILL LAND A MAN ON THE MOON BEFORE THE DECADE IS OUT!

THE US SPACE MISSION WAS TOP PRIORITY AND GOING WELL, EXCEPT FOR A FEW MINOR HICCUPS...

YIKES! WHAT ARE THOSE PARTICLES FLOATING AROUND?

THEY'LL GET INTO THE CONTROLS!

GEE! I'M SURE GLAD I SMUGGLED THIS CORNED BEEF SANDWICH ABOARD! BETTER THAN FOOD CUBES ANY DAY!

MISSION CONTROL THOUGHT OTHERWISE! THE WEIGHTLESSNESS CAUSED CRUMBS TO FLY EVERYWHERE! JOHN YOUNG WAS SEVERELY REPRIMANDED!

ON 20th FEBRUARY 1962, JOHN GLENN BECAME THE FIRST AMERICAN TO ORBIT THE EARTH. IT WAS DURING THE TWO-MAN GEMINI MISSION IN 1965 AND 1966 THAT...

THIS IS IT! I'M OPENING THE HATCH!

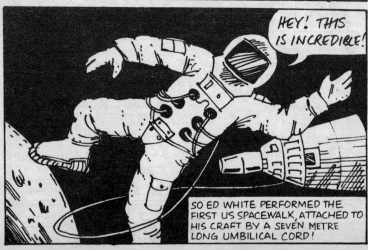

HEY! THIS IS INCREDIBLE!

SO ED WHITE PERFORMED THE FIRST US SPACEWALK, ATTACHED TO HIS CRAFT BY A SEVEN METRE LONG UMBILICAL CORD!

While the Americans had been concentrating on getting to the Moon, Russia had been putting all its efforts into establishing a permanent space station.

The first such station, *Salyut*, was launched on 19 April 1971. By the end of 1977, there were five more, with *Soyuz* craft ferrying visiting crews to and fro.

America, meanwhile, had embarked upon the Space Shuttle programme and made twenty-four flights between 1981 and 1986, when a disaster brought their space transportation systems to a halt. The Russians, however, continued to move forward, and in 1986 they launched *Mir* (meaning 'peace'), the first module of a permanently manned space station with docking ports for up to six spacecraft.

Our fascination with space remains and the story so far is not the end ... only the beginning!

The Science Museum in London has the actual *Apollo* 10 Command Capsule.

**Museums where you can find out more about space:**

Aerospace Museum, Wolverhampton, West Midlands

Museum of Science and Engineering, Newcastle
upon Tyne

Museum of Science and Industry, Birmingham

Museum of the History of Science, Broad Street,
Oxford

Science Museum, Exhibition Road, London SW7

Science Museum, Wroughton, Wiltshire

# IN THE HOME

*T*oday's houses and flats are very different from the homes of our ancestors. In Britain we take for granted such modern inventions as cookers, refrigerators, washing machines and electric lights. Yet all of these were only invented in the last one hundred and fifty years. Try looking at some of the rooms in your home and think about how people lived without all these modern devices.

In the kitchen we prepare and cook food and wash up our plates and cutlery. Cooking used to be done over open fires so the kitchen was very hot and smoky.

---

**FACT**

Huge joints of meat used to be cooked on a spit, a long metal rod with a handle at one end for turning the meat over and over so that it cooked evenly. This is how we get the phrase 'done to a turn'.

---

In 1780, Thomas Robinson developed the first kitchen range. Instead of an open fire with a pot hanging above it and a joint roasting on the spit, an oven and boiler enclosed the fire, and food cooked in the oven. Many people still cooked on an old-fashioned range right up until the First World War.

The first gas cookers were developed in Victorian times. At first they were not popular because it was thought that the food would taste of gas. The first electric cookers were introduced in around 1900. Today most of us at home cook either on gas or electric cookers. However, there is an exciting new oven – the

microwave. This uses rays which heat and cook food much faster than a normal oven. A baked potato takes about one hour in an oven and only 5 minutes in a microwave! Hospitals, pubs, restaurants and airlines, all feeding lots of people, find microwaves very useful.

---

**FACT**

Today we usually eat off plates, using knives and forks. If you had lived in the Middle Ages you had no plate but a 'trencher', a thick slice of stale bread, which was used as a plate. Most people ate with their fingers. The first forks were introduced into Britain in 1601.

---

Keeping food cool so that it does not go off is very important. In the past, the only way to keep meat and fish was to salt it and dry it. There was none of today's tinned and frozen foods, and vegetables and dairy products such as milk and butter could not be kept fresh. Only very grand houses had an ice-house in the garden where big blocks of ice, collected from rivers in the winter, were stored all year round.

The first refrigerators were just boxes with ice in the bottom of them. Then, instead of ice, electric motors were used to keep the re-frigerator cold. Today's fridges use a motor and a special liquid called a coolant, which absorbs the heat in the fridge so that it is cold enough to store all our perishable goods.

## FACT

Emperor Napoleon of France played a part in the development of canned food. He needed large supplies of food to feed his army when it was on the march, so he offered a prize to anyone who could find a way of storing food without it going bad. Nicholas Appet discovered that food could be kept fresh in sealed tin cans. In the 1820s, the first canned goods went on sale. Tin-openers weren't invented until the 1860s, so tins were opened with a hammer and chisel!

The bathroom is for washing ourselves, either in the bath or the shower. Our ancestors did not have bathrooms in their homes and it was much harder for them to keep clean. Water was heated in the kitchen and was carried upstairs in jugs by servants. In Victorian times, people bathed about once a week, often sharing the water, so the last person had to put up with dirty, lukewarm water! With the invention of the gas geyser in 1868 and then the immersion heater, it became possible to have hot water from the taps in the bathroom. Now we can have hot water for bathing any time we like.

> **FACT**
>
> Soap is one of our oldest inventions. We know from archaeological research that the ancient Sumerians were making soap in the year 3,000 BC.

Washing clothes is done by machine, either at home or at the launderette. Traditionally, all clothes were washed by hand in streams or rivers or at a village pump. Then, in the mid-nineteenth century, hand-operated wooden washing-machines were invented. These were wooden tubs with handles to move the clothes round and round. The first electric washing-machines were introduced in 1914. The washing-machines of today offer a choice of programmes for washing many different types of clothes. A tumble-drier dries them and then they are ready to iron. Irons are also powered by electricity, making them easy to use. In the past irons had to be heated with hot coals, or on the kitchen range, and it was difficult to get them to stay hot.

Every room in the house needs lights. In the past, people had only candles and oil lamps and they tended to get up when it was light and go to bed when it was dark. Then two inventors, Joseph Swan and Thomas Edison, both discovered how to make the electric light bulb. Today we can have light all day and all night.

### Did you know?

- The first toothpaste tube was made in 1892. Before then, toothpaste was sold in round ceramic pots. You can often see them in museums.

- The first people to use water-pipes made of lead were the Romans, who spoke Latin. They called the craftsman who installed the pipes a 'plumbarius' or 'worker in lead', hence the word plumber.

- We may not like spring-cleaning, but we are not forced to do it. In Hungary, in 1937, a law was passed that all lofts and cellars had to be spring-cleaned every year or the owner of the house would have to pay a fine.

**Museums where you can find out more about the history of household objects:**

Geffrye Museum, Kingsland Road, London E2

Museum of English Rural Life, Reading, Berkshire

People's Palace, Glasgow Green, Glasgow, Scotland

Science Museum, Exhibition Road, London SW7

Victoria and Albert Museum, Exhibition Road, London SW7

Weald and Downland Open Air Museum, Singleton, Nr Chichester, Sussex

Welsh Folk Museum, St Fagan's, Cardiff, Wales

York Castle Museum, York

Don't forget that National Trust houses provide an opportunity to see historic houses and interiors, usually with original furniture. At Erdigg, an eighteenth-century house in Wrexham, Clwyd, Wales, you can see a working laundry and bakehouse and the servants' quarters as well as all the grand rooms of the house.

The Museum of Mankind and The Commonwealth Institute in London are good places to find out how people live in the different countries of the world.

# CLOTHES

When you go shopping in your local town, you will see many different shops selling clothes and shoes. You may need a pair of jeans and a T-shirt or a grand outfit for a special occasion. The clothes in the shops are all made in factories, using industrial sewing-machines. But for many hundreds of years all clothes were made by hand, at home.

The first clothes worn by humans were the coverings made of fur and animal skins worn by cavemen and women. Then it was discovered that wool from sheep and goats could be spun and woven to make cloth, as could cotton and flax from plants. Woven tunics, called togas, were worn by both men and women in ancient Greece and Rome. All over the world, techniques of dyeing and weaving cloth evolved, and different styles of costume were worn according to climate and custom. Many traditional costumes still survive, though often only worn on ceremonial occasions.

81

In Britain, where the Industrial Revolution started, many new inventions speeded up the spinning and weaving processes. Cloth from Britain was exported all over the world from the mills of Yorkshire and Lancashire. One of the best places to visit today if you want to learn about weaving is the Quarry Bank Mill Museum at Styal in Cheshire, which has many working machines.

Because all clothes were made by hand they had to last a long time. The first sewing-machine was invented by a Frenchman called Barthelemy Thimmonier in 1829. However, when the machine was used to sew uniforms for the army the tailors went on strike and smashed the machines, realizing that their jobs were threatened. The forerunner of today's sewing-machines was designed and patented by an American called Isaac Singer. At the Clyde-bank District Museum in Dumbarton, Scotland, there are hundreds of sewing-machines on display since Singer's in Clydebank was at one time the largest sewing-machine factory in Europe!

If you look at old pictures and photographs, you will see that we have not always dressed the way we dress now. Women and little girls wore dresses to the ground while men have worn all sorts of different-shaped trousers – padded doublet and hose in Elizabethan times and breeches and tailcoats in the nineteenth century. It was not until after the First World War that women's skirts were shortened and the man's modern suit was standardized. Many museums have collections of textiles and costumes and fashion accessories such as fans, parasols, ties and gloves.

**Museums where you can find out more about the history of clothing:**

Gallery of English Costume, Platt Hall, Platt Fields,
 Rusholme, Manchester

Museum of Costume, Assembly Rooms, Bath, Avon

Paisley Museum and Art Gallery, High Street,
 Paisley, Scotland

Rougemont House Museum of Costume and Lace,
 Castle Street, Exeter, Devon

Victoria and Albert Dress Collection, Victoria and
 Albert Museum, Exhibition Road, London SW7

# LIVING DOLLS

Dolls are simply small models of human beings and for thousands of years children have loved and played with them. Most girls, and some boys, have had a doll collection at one time or another and many grown-ups still have their favourite childhood doll. Perhaps your mum or dad still have dolls from when they were children?

Not all dolls were for playing with. The dolls found in the tombs of the ancient Egyptians, buried together with small children, may well have been religious objects rather than playthings. But the ancient Greeks and Romans did have play dolls, some of which can still be seen – in museums of course!

The oldest known dolls – and the ones most prized by collectors – are baked clay figures of some 3,000 years BC. Rag dolls, wooden dolls with beads for hair and clay dolls with movable arms from many centuries ago have been found in ancient graves.

Until the nineteenth century, dolls were always made in the form of women and girls, but now there are some male dolls around – like Action Man.

**FACT**

The making of dolls for sale began in Germany when woodcutters and charcoal-burners started carving them for their own children and then began selling them door-to-door or at fairs. Later, whole families became involved in the work, one family making heads, another legs, and so on. The completed wooden dolls were then sent off to distant towns and countries.

In the sixteenth century came the beautiful fashion dolls, dressed up as miniature ladies of the Paris dressmakers and sent to the European courts to show the latest styles of hairdressing and clothes.

Of course, wooden dolls were rather clumsy and difficult to play with, so in the seventeenth century, dolls were made of rags or leather skins stuffed with sawdust. Next came wax dolls – some with real hair – which were difficult to make because each hair had to be put into the wax with a hot needle. Jointed dolls with hollow bodies followed. They had wire inside so that they could sit and move their arms and legs. After these came dolls that could shut and open their eyes and dolls that could say 'Mama' and 'Papa'. Baby dolls, rather than 'adult' dolls, were the last of all to be introduced.

There are lots of wonderful collections of dolls
in doll and toy museums around the country.
One of these is the Warwick Doll Museum,
which has about 275 dolls as well as many
other miniature figures. Another is Pollock's
Toy Museum in London.

But of course, the best doll of all is your own
special favourite, waiting patiently for you at
home!

**Museums where you can find out more about dolls:**

Bethnal Green Museum of Childhood, London E2

Doll and Toy Museum, Cockermouth, Cumbria

Doll Museum, Warwick, Warwickshire

Finlaystone Doll Collection, Renfrewshire, Scotland

Jacob's Farm Children's Museum, Laxfield, Suffolk

Museum of Childhood, Beaumaris, Gwynedd, Wales

Museum of Childhood, Edinburgh, Scotland

Museum of Dolls, Newark, Nottinghamshire

Precinct Toy Collection, Sandwich, Kent

Teddy Bear Museum, Stratford-upon-Avon,
   Warwickshire

The Museum, Newton Stewart, Wigtown, Scotland

# START YOUR OWN MINI-MUSEUM

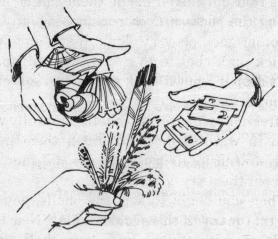

*B*y starting a collection, you are on the first step of the ladder to being a proud owner of your very own mini-museum! You don't need to have lots of money; you can begin by picking up articles like bus tickets, buttons, feathers, grasses or shells – everyday things which you might find lying around near your own home, in the country or at the seaside.

The collections held in museums are carefully displayed and devotedly looked after. You must always remember to treat your own collection in the same way. We are going to look at how to start a shell collection, but many of these ideas can be applied to other objects.

Shells can be found quite easily on many sea-shores around Britain. The best time to look for them is just after a spell of bad weather, when the shells have been thrown high up the beaches by the rough seas. Many of the creatures that once lived inside them can be found among the rocks and in rock-pools – so these are other good places to look. If you *do* happen to pick up a shell with a creature still inside, don't drop it – put it back gently and search for an empty one!

After collecting several shells, carefully wash them in warm water and brush them gently (with an old tooth-brush) to get the sand out, then pat them dry with a towel.

When you begin to sort the shells, you will find that many of them look similar. Nearly all shells are either univalve – one shell only – like the spirally-coiled periwinkle, limpet and garden snail, or bivalve, which have two parts that open up by a little hinge in the middle.

Once you have put your shells together in these groups, you have started to classify them.

You can store your collection in old shoe-boxes, and protect them by using a lining of tissue-paper or cotton wool. If you want people to view your collection, you can display them by fixing them on to a sheet of card. Use Blu-tack or Plasticine – then they can be moved around should you decide to add to or change your display.

The museum experts (called curators) try to find out as much as they possibly can about their collections in order to best inform others. You can do this. Your public or school library is sure to have many books on shells. Try to match up your shells with the pictures in these books and when you have found out the name of each and have identified them, you can put a little name tag beside or below the actual shell.

Once you have started a collection, you'll probably find that you get the collecting bug!

# INDEX